Inside the Seed

Other plays by Jason Patrick Rothery

A Perilous State of Grace
Cat vs. Duck (or, A Literary Evening)
The Drop
Menace
POLITIkO
(re)Birth: e. e. Cummings in Song
Re:Generation (with Aaron Coates, Michaela Jeffrey, and
   THEATREboom)
The Ring Around
Seize the Fish
Something to Do With Death (with Eric Rose, Invisible Elephant, and
   Ghost River Theatre)
the space between us (formerly, *Men without Lips*)
Wedgie (with Upintheair Theatre)
Wilson's Leg

INSIDE
THE SEED

|||||||||||||||||| a play by ||||||||||||||||||

Jason Patrick Rothery

Talonbooks

Talonbooks
278 East First Avenue, Vancouver, British Columbia, Canada V5T 1A6
www.talonbooks.com

First printing: 2016
Printed and bound in Canada on 100% post-consumer recycled paper

Interior design by Chloë Filson
Cover design by Typesmith and Chloë Filson
Cover image of wheat stalk adapted from illustration courtesy Peter H. Raven Library, Missouri Botanical Gardens, via Biodiversity Heritage Library and Flickr (C.C. 2.0)

Talonbooks acknowledges the financial support of the Canada Council for the Arts, the Government of Canada through the Canada Book Fund, and the Province of British Columbia through the British Columbia Arts Council and the Book Publishing Tax Credit.

Library and Archives Canada Cataloguing in Publication

Rothery, Jason Patrick, 1978–, author
            Inside the seed : a play / Jason Patrick Rothery.

"Inside the Seed is a contemporary version of Oedipus Rex
            reimagined as a darkly comic political thriller" – Publisher's note.

Issued also in electronic formats.

ISBN 978-0-88922-986-0 (paperback). – ISBN 978-0-88922-987-7 (epub).
– ISBN 978-1-77201-050-3 (kindle). – ISBN 978-1-77201-051-0 (pdf)

This play is dedicated to my parents,
Michael Rothery and Leslie Tutty.

Our world is defined by those
who fulfill the courage of their convictions.

Introduction

Inside the Seed is an attempt to tell an old story in a new way (which, of course, is what all storytelling is). I fell in love with *Oedipus Rex* in a first-year drama history course. I've always had a penchant for flawed leaders – that strange, complex commingling of benevolence and hubris. I like stories about fate, predestination, free will; stories that probe the extent to which we are masters of our own destinies. *Oedipus Rex* hit me in the head and in the gut, and has remained a personal favourite. When the opportunity arose to adapt a classic, there was no question.

Except for how? How do we retell old stories in new ways? How do we reconfigure a classic? How do we deign to tap into the psyche of an ancient, absent civilization?

Many other authors have, of course, grappled with these same questions. Introducing his beloved adaptation of Seneca's *Oedipus*, Ted Hughes writes that he decided to adapt the Senecan rather than the Sophoclean version because the "Greek world saturates Sophocles too thoroughly: the evolution of his play seems complete, fully explored and ... fully civilized" (8). In this, Hughes evokes Georg Lukács who, in *The Theory of the Novel*, deems the world of Greek drama "all embracing and closed within itself" (46). Lukács distinguishes the fragmented interiority of a protagonist (in a novel) journeying toward an unobtainable coherence, from dramatic heroes who, because they are situated in a pre-constituted and self-contained reality, have "no interiority" (88).

I think that Hughes and Lukács are addressing the same anxiety from different angles: How do we retell stories? If the legitimating stamp of canonization has deemed the Sophoclean version "complete," what right does Hughes have to tinker with (and, what, risk ruining?) this perfectly calibrated machine? In selecting Seneca's version for adaptation, Hughes suggests that only inferior or imperfect iterations are ripe for retelling. The canonical, by comparison, has crystallized and is only available *as is*. Hughes translates reverence into atrophy.

While circling around how different media (say stage and print) facilitate storytelling in different ways, Lukács treats the Greek world as a distant and exotic locale; a foreign topography operating according to arcane and perplexing protocols, ethics, and cognitions. For Lukács, the novel's fractured consciousness is analogous to *his* time and place (the early 20th century): a kaleidoscope of disparate relativism. Any notion of a complete or total reality has shattered and diffused into a subjective splay. How could we possibly understand what our Greek forebears were going on about?

Sophocles was neither the last nor the first to tell the story of Oedipus, solver of the Sphinx's riddle. He took an ancient myth and refashioned it into a searing courtroom drama. (My favourite encapsulation of *Oedipus Rex* comes from a David Mamet-esque sock puppet "movie trailer" concocted by Peter Wilson. The slogan: *Oedipus Rex: Father Killer. Motherfucker.*) While I share Hughes's penchant for Sophocles (despite the undeniable, visceral appeal of Seneca's gore- and viscera-saturated retelling), I reject Hughes's stratification. Every iteration is a point on a continuum. Or, like Lévi-Strauss contends, all versions of a myth comprise a single myth. An ubermyth. Every version, every retelling, enriches the paradigm.

Back to Lukács: How do we account for the alterity of art produced in very different times and places? What does a dramatic device such as a chorus mean to an audience today? How does fatalism jive with the postmodern mind? Will most, if not all, contemporary audiences approach this play as a corollary to Freudian psychoanalysis; that is, the infamous *complex*? This is all to say that a 2,500-year-old play is not simply a window into, or encounter with, the past, but entails an effort to reconcile that past, in all its idiosyncratic glory, with our present. Trying to make the past make sense in the present (or, as we tend to say, making the material *relevant*) is a perpetual concern. This is the lodestar animating endeavours such as "original practices" Shakespeare. But the project is a fallacy. First, because we will we only recover *select* practices – those that will least offend the comfort and sensitivities of present-day audiences – and second, because by emulating the past we only underscore its distance from us. How do we recover the past without pushing it away?

Not to presume that my own approach is universally applicable, I decided to use *Oedipus Rex* as a template. I did not want to dis- and re-assemble Sophocles, but tried to build something different with his blueprint and see if the structure would stand. As such, *Inside the Seed* is and isn't *Oedipus Rex*. Some people see the parallels, some don't, and it doesn't matter to me either way. Early on I began to parse which components to retain or jettison – an admittedly subjective call. I didn't know how to make the chorus work for my purposes (though Richard Wolfe, the director of the premiere production, certainly did; basically, Richard kept all of the actors on stage for the whole show and used breath and physical gestures to underscore key moments). In *Oedipus Rex*, I was intrigued by the form: the single location and timeline; that runaway-train / free-fall feeling. I got snagged on an element of the play that slides by with little comment: Oedipus is himself the source of the plague. This correlation between moral and physical corruption would have resonated with a Greek audience in a particular way, but could it take on new relevance in a contemporary context? I wanted to explore the responsibility of the ruler – both arrogant and well-intentioned – to the ruled. Working in the wake of President Obama's first election, I thought a lot about sacrifice. What sacrifices do our leaders ask of us? What sacrifices are we *willing* to make? The subprime mortgage crisis emanated echoes of the Enron scandal of the early 2000s. Watch Enron's erstwhile CEO Jeffrey Skilling testify before Congress (or any interview with Dick Cheney, ever), and tell me that we human beings don't have a highly evolved capacity for self-delusion. I studied seeds and GMO foods. I started out on one extreme of the debate, but as research proceeded, I was drawn further and further toward the murky middle – that vast swath of grey.

All of which is a roundabout way of saying that instead of attempting to emulate the past through aesthetics or practices, I'm far more interested in a conversation with that past. A conversation between stories. Like all forms of life, stories have a morphology that depends simultaneously on deeply ingrained structures and the local conditions in which any given entity grows. Both this structure and these conditions are fundamental to the success of any species. Structures evolve. Conditions change. As stories disseminate, they carry with them traces of their lineage, their past lives, of all the versions that came before, while adapting to new contexts in order to survive. Every story is a story of survival and adaptation. Every story is a version of other stories. Every story is a seed. The more stories, the more versions; the more verdant and replenished our world.

—Jason Patrick Rothery

Production History

Inside the Seed was first produced in the VanCity Culture Lab at the Vancouver East Cultural Centre, October 2 to 12, 2013, with the following cast and crew:

FOSTER BRYANT – Patrick Sabongui

AVA – Alison Raine

ISOBEL BRYANT – Mia K. Ingimundson

COLE – Carl Kennedy

SUSAN FARMER – Tamara McCarthy

GERSON – Dave Mott

DR. VANDALIA GILROY – Adele Noronha

SAMPSON PAI – Tetsuro Shigematsu

ALEX SKILLING – Dallas Sauer

Directed by Richard Wolfe

Direction assistance by Daniel Martin

Set and lighting designed by Jergus Oprsal

Costumes designed by Florence Barrett

Sound designed by Jordan Watkins

Produced by Upintheair Theatre

Cast of Characters

FOSTER BRYANT, mid-thirties, Demetech's CEO, manufacturer of Golden Grain

AVA, Foster's assistant

ISOBEL BRYANT, early forties, Foster's pregnant wife, Eastern European background

COLE, Demetech's CFO, of African descent

SUSAN FARMER, forties, farmer

GERSON, Cole's former army buddy, now a senator's aide

DR. VANDALIA GILROY, GMO activist, of South Asian descent

SAMPSON PAI, former Demetech research scientist, of Asian descent

ALEX SKILLING, journalist

Various other characters, including a SECURITY GUARD and two MEN hanging a painting

Inside the Seed

The power of population is so superior to the power of the earth to produce subsistence for man that premature death must in some shape or other visit the human race. The vices of mankind are active and able ministers of depopulation. They are the precursors in the great army of destruction, and often finish the dreadful work themselves. But should they fail in this war of extermination, sickly seasons, epidemics, pestilence, and plague advance in terrific array, and sweep off their thousands and tens of thousands. Should success be still incomplete, gigantic inevitable famine stalks in the rear, and with one mighty blow levels the population with the food of the world.

—Thomas Malthus
An Essay on the Principle of Population (1798)

She trapped herself; she marched into the labyrinth of her own construction. Her doubts could be neutralized only by plunging in deeper.

—Ian McEwan
Atonement (2001)

In the darkness ...

GILROY

(*voiceover*) The problem, Mr. Bryant, is that you do not know, nor care to know, the limits of your own understanding. You see only what you want to see; look only for what you want to find ...

> *Lights up. We are in FOSTER's office – sleek and elegant, one door in and out. There is a wide desk with a computer and a phone. In front of the desk is a long conference table surrounded by chairs. Everything is ultra-modern – steel and glass. Through giant windows a great city glistens below.*
>
> *Beneath the polished facade there are cracks; subtle indications that the foundation is not solid; the exterior glow masks the interior rot.*
>
> *FOSTER is seated at his desk. He is wearing a headset and staring at his monitor. Two MEN are perched on a ladder hanging a large painting on the wall behind him – The Massacre of the Innocents by Peter Paul Rubens.*
>
> *FOSTER clicks his mouse, listening and re-listening to a recording of GILROY's statement.*

GILROY

(*voiceover*) You see only what you want to see; look only for what you want to find ... (*click*) You see only what you want to see; look only for what you want to find ... (*click*) You see only what you want to see; look only for what you want to –

> *Click. The voice cuts out.*

FOSTER

(*into headset*) Still here. New building, new wiring, still sorting out all the bugs ... (*listening*) Connecting every machine to every other machine ... (*listening*) The last I heard was Paul ... (*listening*) Paul was asking about Africa ... (*listening*) Yes, the same three countries still refuse to take the aid ... (*listening*) Zambia, Zimbabwe, and Mozambique ... (*listening*) The quote? The quote came from the prime minister of Mozambique ... (*listening*) They have a prime minister and a president ... (*listening*) It's a republic ... (*listening*) "Simply because people are hungry is not justification for feeding them poison" ... (*listening*) "Poison" ... (*listening*) That's the quote ... (*listening*) Yes, she is referring to Golden Grain ... (*listening*) I doubt it was an error in translation ... (*listening*) They will accept the aid. I guarantee they will ... (*listening*) Because I have a plan ... (*listening*) The planes are being loaded as we speak. As soon as I give General Keyes the all clear –

He bangs on the wall for AVA.

FOSTER

I'd rather not go into the details. What's next on the agenda?

AVA enters. FOSTER beckons her over.

FOSTER

(*into headset*) I've met with Duncan regarding the lawsuit and he says he's on top of it. (*covering the headset with his hand and pointing at the screen*) (*to AVA*) This number right here – this is the number of hits? Of people who have watched the clip?

AVA

Yes.

FOSTER

Nineteen thousand?

AVA

That's actually not very many by Internet standards.

FOSTER

It was less than three hundred last night.

AVA

Stop watching it. You're obsessed.

FOSTER

I'm not obsessed. (*back to the headset*) Her name is Farmer. That's right – Farmer. (*laughing*) The timing is unfortunate ...

> *FOSTER mimes drinking a glass of water. AVA gives him a thumbs-up, exits.*

FOSTER

(*into headset*) Duncan is shifting any civil litigation that predates the merger to a subsidiary. It's contained. Fallout should be negligible. Anything else?

> *AVA enters with a glass of water.*

FOSTER

(*into headset*) What article?

> *AVA turns and exits.*

FOSTER

(*into headset*) What magazine?

> *AVA enters with the water and a magazine. FOSTER takes the magazine.*

FOSTER

(*into headset*) Uh-huh ... (*listening*) uh-huh ... (*listening*) yeah ... (*covering the headset, to AVA*) When did this come out?

AVA

Two days ago.

FOSTER

(*back to the headset*) *Fortune* magazine.

AVA

(*whispering*) Cole said not to tell you.

FOSTER

(*into headset*) Alex Skilling? Never heard of him. Never talked to him. (*beat*) If I'd talked to him, I'd remember.

AVA

Sorry!

FOSTER *shoos her out.*

FOSTER

(*into headset*) Am I quoted? ... (*listening*) Is Cole quoted? ... (*listening*) Is *anyone* quoted? Then he didn't – what? Skilling – did he contact anyone? Did he make any effort to get our side of the – (*listening*) He doesn't know how our company makes money? What does that even mean? ... (*listening*) I think these questions are better put to Cole. He's the numbers guy. You know how my eyes glaze over when – Yeah ... (*laughing*) No comment!

The MEN *use a laser level to check that the painting is hung straight.*

FOSTER

(*into headset*) Before we go, I wanted to express my gratitude to all of you for your hard work and dedication to this company, to *our* company ... everything you've done to bring this project to fruition. We're going to feed the world. How's that for a legacy? ... (*listening*) That's very kind of you to say. I think he would have been as well. Same to you.

He hangs up, removes the headset, and takes a deep breath.
AVA enters.

AVA
> Your wife is here.

FOSTER
> You knew about this? The article?

AVA
> Cole said not to tell you.

FOSTER
> You don't work for Cole.

AVA
> I know.

FOSTER
> Where is he?

AVA
> I don't know.

FOSTER
> Can you find him?

AVA
> I'll find him. Should I send him up if I find him?

FOSTER
> If you find him, yes, please send him up.

AVA
> Your wife is here.

FOSTER
> And track down this ... Alex Skilling. Call him. Ask him to come in.

AVA

Okay. Who is Alex Skilling again?

FOSTER

The reporter from *Fortune*. The author of the –

AVA

Gotcha.

AVA exits.

MAN

We're done.

FOSTER

Appreciate it.

The MEN exit. FOSTER takes a moment to breathe in his new office and admire the painting.

ISOBEL enters. She delivers her dialogue in an Eastern European accent.

ISOBEL

You could not let it go.

FOSTER

Pookie! Sweet-cheeks! Muffin-face!

ISOBEL

You bought it.

FOSTER

Bought what?

ISOBEL

This. That. It. The –

FOSTER

It?

ISOBEL
It. It!

FOSTER
You don't like it?

ISOBEL
Ugh!

FOSTER
You dismiss this … this masterpiece with a single syllable?

ISOBEL
Precisely the response it requires. An "Ah!" or an "Ew!" or an "Eek!"

FOSTER
You're so wrong.

ISOBEL
How much did you pay?

FOSTER
Beside the point.

ISOBEL
One million? Ten?

FOSTER
You can't put a price on genius.

ISOBEL
More than fifty? Foster! One hundred? Not more than one hundred, please!

Beat.

FOSTER
One seventeen.

ISOBEL

One hundred and seventeen million? You fool!

FOSTER

It's not my fault you lack the sophistication to appreciate the classics.

ISOBEL

It is relentless, remorseless, childishly macabre. All sinew and no soul. It exists only *to be seen*. It serves no purpose but to make us stand here, struck dumb in awe.

FOSTER

And I say the world needs more awe.

ISOBEL

It is grotesque. Both it itself and what you paid.

FOSTER

Your father must have more expensive pieces.

ISOBEL

But he is rich, and you are not.

FOSTER

Isobel, I didn't buy it. The company did.

ISOBEL

Not rich like him. Not yet, my love.

FOSTER

It's for the building. Decor.

ISOBEL

Also my father has taste.

    Beat.

FOSTER

Give me your purse.

ISOBEL

My which?

FOSTER

Your purse. Your bag.

ISOBEL

It's a satchel.

FOSTER

Your satchel then. Give it over.

She hands him the satchel. He opens it, rummages around …

FOSTER

Aha!

Like a magic trick, FOSTER pulls a Harlequin romance out of the satchel.

FOSTER

Queen of the Isle.

ISOBEL

Foster!

FOSTER

(*reading*) "Tyrell's anger burst into flame like a struck match and was extinguished just as quickly. 'Do you still favour white roses?' he asked, his voice as dry as autumn leaves. Joan shot him a pointed look, but inside her resolve was wilting. 'Of course I do. You know I do.' His lips curled into a sneer. 'Never forget.' "

ISOBEL

Give it back! How dare you!

FOSTER

(*reading*) "Joan's eyes fluttered, her skin pricked as the air was charged with sexual tension. She turned away from Tyrell and clung to the banister as she moistened her lips with the tip of her tongue" –

ISOBEL snatches back the book and satchel.

ISOBEL

My indulgence cost five bucks at the airport.

She stuffs the book inside the satchel, retrieves a pack of cigarettes, and lights one.

FOSTER

Izzy, don't.

ISOBEL

Don't "don't" me, Foster.

She puffs twice then stubs out the cigarette.

FOSTER

Why do you even bother?

ISOBEL

It is the ritual I miss, not the smoke itself. (*beat*) No smokes, no booze, no drugs … If I had known pregnancy was such a bore I never would have bothered. (*beat*) I didn't mean it, darling. I am cranky, okay? Too much poking and prodding. Needle after needle. More tests today. These endless tests!

FOSTER

He's not treating you any differently.

ISOBEL

Don't lie to me, Foster. I know you order more for me. Why deny this? Because of my age. Because of the risks for a woman my age.

FOSTER

It has nothing to do with your –

ISOBEL

Foster, spare me. Of course it is my age. I am not ashamed. They *should* give me more tests. I need them, obviously.

FOSTER

We're taking extra precautions. That's all.

ISOBEL

There is no guarantee, you know? They can give me every test there is, and still …

FOSTER

How did you feel this morning?

ISOBEL

I was throwing up, but this is comforting. It means that everything is in order. You are coming with me? To the doctor?

　　Beat.

FOSTER

Izzy, I can't.

ISOBEL

But you said you would.

FOSTER

I said I'd see –

ISOBEL

You said –

FOSTER

I'd see what I could do.

　　Beat.

ISOBEL

Not much.

FOSTER

I'm shipping one hundred thousand tonnes of grain to Africa today. Not the ideal time to go traipsing out to the –

ISOBEL

Traipsing?!

FOSTER

Isobel, hold on, that's not –

ISOBEL

Three years of tests, procedures … did I mention needles? Awful moments – we despaired you and I – and this is all now … what?

FOSTER

I want to be there. You know I want to –

ISOBEL

Traipsing!

FOSTER

But I can't. Not today.

ISOBEL

Have it your way.

FOSTER

Don't pout.

ISOBEL

I don't pout! (*beat*) Foster, we once thought we would never get this far.

FOSTER

I know.

ISOBEL

What if this child is not meant to be?

> *Beat.*

FOSTER

Will they do an ultrasound?

ISOBEL

(*brightening*) Yes! My first ultrasound. I need water. They told me to
come with bladder full and not to pee.

He gives her his glass of water. She chugs it.

FOSTER

Will they be able to see? The sex?

ISOBEL

Sixteen weeks for that. A little early yet.

FOSTER

But only by a week or two …

ISOBEL

I do not want to know, Foster. I want it to be a surprise.

Beat.

FOSTER

All right. Me too.

ISOBEL

Ha!

FOSTER

"Ha"?

ISOBEL

You will want to know, have to know. You want a boy. All men want
boys. When they can see the sex you will not be able to resist.

FOSTER

You doubt my restraint?

ISOBEL

Indeed I do.

FOSTER

Well we'll see who gets the last laugh.

ISOBEL laughs. FOSTER sweeps her into a kiss …

ISOBEL

(*referring to the painting*) Why do you like it so much?

FOSTER

Like what so much?

ISOBEL

It. Your cloud.

FOSTER

Because … He's trying to save them.

ISOBEL

But this is a massacre. Herod's men have come to take the children away to be slaughtered.

FOSTER

That's not what I see. (*beat*) Cole likes it.

ISOBEL

Cole is a philistine.

FOSTER

Subjective.

ISOBEL

And he lies to please you.

FOSTER

What's wrong with that?

ISOBEL

He has yet to congratulate me.

FOSTER
For what?

ISOBEL
The pregnancy! He has not said congratulations.

FOSTER
He must have.

ISOBEL
. He has not! (*beat*) How do you call for Ava?

FOSTER
Ava!

    AVA enters.

AVA
Yes?

ISOBEL
Ava, there is a liquor store across the street.

AVA
I know it well.

ISOBEL
Go there and buy two bottles of red wine.

FOSTER
Don't send her out on errands. She's busy!

ISOBEL
I wish to conduct an experiment. It will not take long, darling, promise.

AVA
I *am* pretty busy.

ISOBEL

Two bottles of wine – both the most expensive and least expensive bottle they have in stock.

AVA

Okay.

ISOBEL

When you return, pour out the expensive bottle –

AVA

Pour it out where?

ISOBEL

No matter. Pour it out, and refill it with the cheap wine. Yes?

FOSTER

Izzy, what are you up to?

ISOBEL

When Cole arrives, bring in the expensive bottle filled with the cheap wine. Three glasses. Yes?

AVA

Expensive bottle, cheap wine, three glasses – check.

ISOBEL

Tell me, Ava, what do you think of this painting?

AVA

It's dark.

ISOBEL

Go.

    AVA exits.

ISOBEL

Dark and hung crooked.

FOSTER

I know a laser level that says you're wrong.

ISOBEL

What is this laser?

FOSTER

A concentrated beam of light.

ISOBEL

And I am not?

FOSTER

Not what?

ISOBEL

A beam of light! The sun, you said! My sun and moon ... You said
these things to me!

FOSTER

That's what we call pillow talk.

ISOBEL

I say it's crooked.

FOSTER

As you wish.

They kiss.

ISOBEL

Let's do it.

FOSTER

Do what?

ISOBEL

You know ... It. *It!*

FOSTER

I don't think so.

ISOBEL

Yes. Here. We will – what? – *christen* your new office!

FOSTER

No!

She sits on the table seductively.

FOSTER

"Tyrell's anger burst into flame like a struck match, and was extinguished just as quickly." (*drily*) "Do you still favour white roses?"

ISOBEL

(*startled*) "I do. You know I do."

FOSTER

(*sneering*) "Never forget …"

ISOBEL

(*clinging to the table, moistening her lips*) "Oh Tyrell!" ·

FOSTER goes to her as COLE, Demetech's CFO, opens the door.

COLE

Am I interrupting?

ISOBEL

Cole!

COLE

Ava wasn't outside, so …

ISOBEL

So good to see you!

Greets COLE with a kiss on both cheeks.

ISOBEL

You must be so excited! So proud and excited about your new
building.

COLE

Hard to believe we started out with five thousand dollars and
a garage.

FOSTER

Half a garage.

ISOBEL

And now – big company, new building, fancy furniture …

COLE

We spared no expense.

ISOBEL

And his painting – Foster surprised me – the Rubens …

COLE

Fantastic, don't you think?

ISOBEL

He said you were fond of it.

COLE

Yes. It's so … potent.

ISOBEL

Yes. Potent.

Her cellphone rings.

ISOBEL

I beg your pardon … (*fishing the phone out of her satchel and
answering it*) Hello? *Da, Pietre. Naravno da sam pročitala …*

ISOBEL moves to a corner and continues her conversation.

COLE

How much did it cost?

FOSTER

One seventeen.

COLE

I told you not to spend so much.

FOSTER

If the board gives you any shit just tell them that I am this company.
Tell them that what I want, the company wants.

COLE

Sure. They'll love that.

ISOBEL

Ciao.

She hangs up. AVA enters with a bottle of red wine and three glasses.

FOSTER

That was fast.

ISOBEL

Ah! Superb!

ISOBEL pours three glasses of wine. She hands one to COLE, one to FOSTER, and keeps one for herself.

FOSTER

Ava, won't you join us?

AVA

I'm a gin-and-tonic kinda gal.

She exits.

ISOBEL

Cole, my father always celebrates special occasions with a bottle of this wine.

ISOBEL displays the bottle to COLE. FOSTER attempts to signal something to him.

COLE

Yes … I think I've heard of it.

ISOBEL

It is considered among the best wines in the world. It is *very* expensive.

She raises her glass. COLE follows suit.

ISOBEL

Cole, Foster – a toast to your success! To Golden Grain!

COLE

To Africa!

FOSTER

Salut.

COLE drinks. FOSTER takes a small sip. ISOBEL spits her mouthful back into her glass.

ISOBEL

The pregnancy, you know. I am not allowed.

COLE

Mmm … delicious …

ISOBEL

You like it?

COLE

Very much.

ISOBEL

I thought you would.

FOSTER

Sometimes I really don't get your sense of humour.

ISOBEL

I'm Eastern European, I do not have a sense of humour.

They kiss.

ISOBEL

Cole, adieu.

ISOBEL sets down her glass and exits. COLE takes another sip of wine.

COLE

Nice wine.

FOSTER takes COLE's glass and sets all three glasses aside.

FOSTER

She said you haven't congratulated her.

COLE

For what?

FOSTER

The baby.

COLE

I don't understand why we congratulate pregnant people. You had unprotected sex and nature took its course. *Not* getting someone pregnant, *that's* the challenge. I should be applauded every time my girlfriend gets her period.

FOSTER

You have a girlfriend?

COLE

What's up with you?

FOSTER

What? Nothing.

COLE

What's that look on your face?

FOSTER

What look?

COLE

All flushed cheeks and shit-eating grin ... You look like a teenager who just got his first blowjob. (*beat*) Foster, did you just get your first blowjob?

FOSTER

Tell me about this article. In *Fortune*.

COLE

(*calling to* AVA) I told you not to tell him!

AVA

(*offstage*) I didn't!

FOSTER

Don't tell her not to tell me stuff.

AVA

(*offstage*) Sorry!

COLE

Some kid – Alan ... Alex ...

FOSTER

Skilling.

COLE

Skilling, right. Called around asking for interviews. I told him
to submit his questions prior, then I get this email full of crazy
shit about our financial statements, stock valuation, accounting
abnormalities –

FOSTER

Abnormalities?

COLE

I told him I'd be happy to help him understand the questions he was
asking and never heard back.

FOSTER

Why didn't you tell me about this?

COLE

Because I didn't want you to go and get all puffed up.

FOSTER

I don't get all puffed up.

COLE

Reporters throw rocks to provoke a reaction. He wants to make a
name for himself and we're an easy target.

FOSTER

If a magazine of this pedigree calls us out, that's going to throw up a
few red flags, don't you think?

COLE

What I'm saying is let me worry about Skilling and you keep your
eyes on the prize. Don't get all puffed up!

FOSTER

I'm not puffed up! I want to know what's going on!

COLE

Fair enough.

FOSTER

I'm trying to rehabilitate our brand.

COLE

I know.

FOSTER

Most people still think Demetech is a chemical company.

COLE

What did I tell you to do, Foster? What did I *beg* you to do?

FOSTER

Change the name.

COLE

And what did you do?

FOSTER

Kept the name.

COLE

What's the first thing you think of when I say "Philip Morris"?

FOSTER

Tobacco.

COLE

What's the first thing you think of when I say the "Altria Group"?

FOSTER

What's the Altria Group?

COLE

It's Philip Morris! They changed their name!

FOSTER

Demetech funded the original research … when we created Golden Grain. I want to run – *that* Demetech – Demetech before it turned to the dark side.

COLE

Don't explain yourself to me. I'm used to your making decisions that
cause the most amount of grief for everyone involved.

FOSTER

Our finances are in order?

COLE

They're under control.

FOSTER

Our stock is solid?

COLE

Better than solid – it's going up!

FOSTER

Okay, that's all I need to know.

COLE

Once Africa is complete, our contracts kick in, we're free and clear.
Speaking of which – what's the word on the shipment?

FOSTER

They're loading the planes as we speak.

COLE

Great. And they're taking off when?

FOSTER

As soon as I talk to Keyes ... once I've given him the signal or ...
the go-ahead or green light or whatever.

COLE

Great. (*beat*) Is he calling you or are you –

FOSTER

He's calling me.

COLE

Great. (*beat*) And that's just a formality, right? Giving him the go-ahead? There's nothing going on that could in any way whatsoever conceivably delay –

FOSTER

I want them all.

COLE

Foster, no.

FOSTER

The governments of Zambia, Zimbabwe, and Mozambique must accept the aid. Not one plane takes off until they do.

COLE

Foster, we've been over this!

FOSTER

I want them all.

COLE

We're talking about people who believe AIDS is spread by evil spirits. If they think the seed is poison then there's nothing you can do to convince them otherwise.

FOSTER

I have a plan. A sort of a plan.

COLE

A sort of a plan? What sort of a plan?

FOSTER

I'd rather not go into the details.

	Beat.

COLE

May I ask you to reconsider?

FOSTER

Yes.

COLE

Will you reconsider?

FOSTER

No.

COLE

I'm naming my first ulcer after you. (*beat*) You taking lunch?

FOSTER

I'm pretty wall-to-wall.

COLE

I'm meeting an old army buddy ... up from Washington. Come with.

FOSTER

Can't do it.

COLE

He's only here for the day. Can you see him this afternoon?

FOSTER

Wait, is this just lunch or is he after something?

COLE

He saw you on TV and thinks you're cute.

FOSTER

You know I don't like military types. They make me antsy.

COLE

He isn't military anymore, he's government.

FOSTER

Perfect! Does he skin puppies alive in his spare time? Because that would be a trifecta!

COLE

I know it's short notice but he asked if I could set something up, so …

AVA enters.

FOSTER

Talk to Ava.

AVA

Susan Farmer is here.

COLE

Does Foster have any time today?

AVA

No.

COLE

But you could squeeze something in?

AVA

No.

COLE

If I asked nicely?

AVA

No.

COLE

If I threatened to fire you?

AVA

(*to FOSTER*) Does he have the authority to fire me?

FOSTER

No.

AVA

(*to COLE*) Then no.

COLE

(*to FOSTER*) He's only down for the day.

FOSTER

(*to AVA*) Can you sort something out?

AVA

Fine. Susan Farmer is here.

COLE

Who's Susan Farmer? Wait, is that the lady from the lawsuit?

FOSTER

Yes.

COLE

The farmer?

FOSTER

Yes.

COLE

The farmer who's suing us?

FOSTER

Yes.

COLE

Her name is Susan Farmer?

FOSTER

Yeah.

COLE

You don't think that's funny?

FOSTER

No.

COLE

(*to AVA*) You?

AVA

Not really.

COLE

(*to FOSTER*) Where's Duncan?

FOSTER

No idea.

COLE

But he's on his way?

FOSTER

Not that I'm aware of.

COLE

Foster, please tell me that you have invited our head of legal counsel to attend the meeting between you and the farmer who is suing us.

FOSTER

I'm keeping lawyers out of it for now.

COLE

May I ask you to reconsider?

FOSTER

Ava, show her in.

> *AVA exits.*

FOSTER

It was hard for us ... Izzy and I ... to conceive. It might look easy from the outside, but for women past a certain age ... and in vitro has its own set of concerns ...

COLE

I know. (*beat*) Congratulations.

FOSTER

Don't congratulate me, congratulate her!

> *AVA enters with SUSAN FARMER, who is pushing a baby stroller. The child is covered with a blanket.*

SUSAN

I thought we said no lawyers.

COLE

I'm not his lawyer. I'm –

FOSTER

Leaving.

> *COLE takes his wine and exits.*

AVA

Mrs. Farmer, this is Mr. Bryant.

FOSTER

How do you do?

SUSAN

Fine. Tired.

FOSTER

Would you care for something to drink?

SUSAN

No, thank you.

FOSTER

A glass of water?

SUSAN

No.

AVA exits. FOSTER offers SUSAN a seat. She sits.

SUSAN

Might I trouble you to keep your voice down?

FOSTER

Of course.

SUSAN

She doesn't sleep well. Or often.

> *Beat.*

FOSTER

Thank you for agreeing to see me.

SUSAN

My husband doesn't think it'll accomplish anything, and my lawyer nearly had a heart attack.

FOSTER

And you? Why did you decide to come?

SUSAN

Because I think if someone accuses you of something, you ought to get to look them in the eye.

FOSTER

I appreciate your candour.

SUSAN

My family have been farmers going back more generations than most families can count. Four years ago, when we found out Demetech was planting test crops adjacent to our land, we got nervous. We'd heard stories. Someone called to assure us you were taking all necessary precautions ... said you built a buffer zone to prevent contamination. (*beat*) That was the word they used. "Contamination." (*beat*) Next harvest, when our crop came to yield, one out of every five plants had that orange hue. Your rice. Your Golden Grain. Year after that, it was more than half. Strange flowers too ... weird hairs and petals. We called to let you know your buffer zone broke down. We saw this as our duty as your neighbours. Then your people showed up. Your ... investigators. Said we stole the seed ... threatened to take us to court. We told them it could have been the wind or ... or bird droppings, but they didn't believe us. We own this seed, they said. Our lawyer told us it would cost at least a million dollars to take the case to trial. So we paid your fine – we had no choice – signed your contract. We agreed to grow your crop and pay your fees and use your chemicals.

FOSTER

May I interject?

SUSAN

I've had five children, Mr. Bryant. Five perfectly healthy children. But then, after your rice contaminated our field ... (*pulling a sheaf of papers out of her purse*) Demetech manufactures some of the most toxic chemicals on earth –

FOSTER

We make no such chemicals. Not anymore.

SUSAN

Heart and liver disease, nervous system disorders, physical deformities –

FOSTER

Mrs. Farmer –

SUSAN

I've done research. For the past year I've done nothing but research.

FOSTER

Please allow me to clarify your information.

    Beat.

SUSAN

Clarify away.

FOSTER

This Demetech, *my* Demetech, is not the company that made
those chemicals. We did not send those people to your farm.
Not intentionally.

SUSAN

You sent them there by accident?

FOSTER

Years ago, Demetech funded research into plant and seed hybrids,
including a project I worked on as a grad student. We created Golden
Grain. It's beta carotene. We tell the plant to move the beta carotene
from the stalk and leaves into the grain itself. It's perfectly safe and
very healthy. So healthy and easy to produce it could save millions
of lives every year. But Demetech abandoned the project to focus
on making chemicals. I started my own company, and that company
was so successful that a few years back I bought Demetech and
shifted the focus back to plants and seeds; back to Golden Grain.
This transition wasn't easy. There were conflicts with personnel
here ... and unfortunately some pre-existing practices continued
amid the confusion.

SUSAN

This test crop ... was it planted before or after you took over?

FOSTER

The point I'm trying to make is –

SUSAN

Before or after?

> *Beat.*

FOSTER

After, but I can assure you –

SUSAN

You buy this company, no matter what harm it's done, then you turn
around and say: No, wait! We're not them! They're not us!

FOSTER

That isn't at all what I'm saying. I don't want to approach this type of
dispute from a litigious –

SUSAN

Your buffer zone broke down! Your seed took over my crop. Now I'm
forced to grow your grain –

FOSTER

We don't want to punish farmers who haven't done anything wrong –

SUSAN

Forced to buy the chemicals to treat the crop we didn't want –

FOSTER

We spend over two million dollars a day on research alone –

SUSAN

Dump waste in landfills, down storm drains, in streams –

FOSTER

Invest in technologies to make these new seeds –

SUSAN

Move along and leave your mess behind –

FOSTER

The right to protect our investment –

SUSAN

You contaminated my land!

FOSTER

Mrs. Farmer, please calm –

SUSAN

You contaminated *me*!

The baby starts to cry. She rocks the stroller back and forth.

SUSAN

Five perfectly healthy babies, then this ... This is what happens, Mr. Bryant, when you trespass into realms that belong to God and God alone.

Beat.

FOSTER

So many times I've heard that God made the world as is – signed and sealed – *complete*. Time and time again I've heard how my tampering is an affront to His work. And yet we've been tinkering with the building blocks of Creation for thousands of years. Corn was once a useless grass with a cob the size of your thumb. You own a dog? You think God made the poodle? I believe in nature. Nature is a code, a system, a series of riddles. We get better at cracking this code, solve more of these riddles, and improve upon nature's less perfect predecessors.

SUSAN

And my daughter? Is she such an improvement?

SUSAN lifts the blanket covering the stroller. FOSTER looks. The baby stops crying.

SUSAN

Now tell me your chemicals are safe. (*replacing the blanket*) You can't say she's a beautiful baby. She is ... in so many ways ... but you can't say that, can you?

Beat.

FOSTER

I'm sorry. About that – before – speaking over each other like that. (*beat*) My wife. She's expecting. We're expecting.

SUSAN

How many do you have?

FOSTER

This will be our first.

SUSAN

Congratulations, Mr. Bryant.

FOSTER

Susan, everything I've done, my whole life's work, hinges on this grain being safe to grow and eat. We've spent years testing both the seed and the products required to treat that seed, and if they aren't safe, I want to know.

SUSAN

My husband likes it … likes the taste of it. He says: We grow it now, we may as well eat it. I won't touch the stuff. You can't know what it's like for me not to be able to eat what I grow.

FOSTER

But I do. Susan, you and I, we have the same mission. We're both trying to feed the world. (*beat*) Give me some time to talk to my people. If you don't like what I find, or you think I'm being dishonest, then sue me. I'll see that you receive a generous settlement.

SUSAN

I don't care about a settlement. I want to know what happened to my daughter.

FOSTER

So do I. You have my word.

Beat.

SUSAN

I'll tell my lawyer to sit tight.

FOSTER extends a hand.

SUSAN

I have your word. That's good enough.

FOSTER

Where are you staying?

SUSAN

The Marriott.

FOSTER

Ava!

AVA enters.

AVA

You bellowed?

FOSTER

Would you please contact the Marriott and have Mrs. Farmer transferred to their best available room.

SUSAN

I like the room I have just fine. (*taking hold of the stroller*) God is the gardener, Mr. Bryant. Nature is the soil for His seed.

SUSAN exits.

AVA

Is she okay?

FOSTER

I don't know.

AVA

Should I phone the Marriott?

FOSTER

Leave it alone. (*beat*) I should eat.

AVA

Mr. Gerson is waiting to see you.

FOSTER

Who's that?

AVA

Cole's buddy.

FOSTER

Can it wait?

AVA

You told me to sort something out!

    Beat.

FOSTER

Send him in.

AVA

You want I should grab you a sandwich?

FOSTER

Naw. Leave it.

    AVA shows GERSON into the office. He carries a suitcase.

AVA

Mr. Gerson, this is Mr. Bryant.

FOSTER

Good to meet you.

GERSON

Likewise. Thanks for taking the time.

FOSTER

Can I offer you something to drink?

GERSON

You can offer.

Beat.

FOSTER

Do you want something to drink?

GERSON

No, but thanks for asking.

AVA exits.

FOSTER

Cole said you're here from Washington?

GERSON

For the day.

FOSTER

The train?

GERSON

I like the drive.

FOSTER

Sorry if I kept you waiting.

GERSON

I never booked an appointment, so you couldn't have kept me waiting.

FOSTER

Fair enough.

GERSON

Just to be clear, I never booked an appointment.

FOSTER

I ... don't know what that means.

GERSON

    I appreciate your discretion is all.

    Beat.

FOSTER

    How do you know Cole?

GERSON

    Black Sheep – Second Platoon, Alpha Company, Second Ranger
    Battalion. We served in the Gulf together.

FOSTER

    My condolences.

GERSON

    (*laughing*) Haven't seen him in a while. Seems to have done all right
    for himself. Certainly done all right by you.

FOSTER

    How so?

GERSON

    He's notorious up on the Hill. Fought hard for you, for your
    company. Loud and clear: our technology is no different from
    good old-fashioned crossbreeding. That what you do down here?
    Crossbreed pea pods with high-tech tools?

FOSTER

    What's your day job, Mr. Gerson?

GERSON

    Thought Cole would have told you. I'm senior aide to Senator
    Orrin Jakes.

FOSTER

    Jakes … I think I met him once.

GERSON
You testified before him at a hearing.

FOSTER
Ah. Yes. He wasn't very nice to me as I recall.

GERSON
Those hearings tend to get a little heated. No hard feelings I hope.

FOSTER
What can I do for the honourable senator?

GERSON
Orrin was recently appointed chair of the Armed Services
Committee.

FOSTER
Like, weapons and stuff?

GERSON
Weapons among other … yes … stuff. Army, navy, air force –

FOSTER
Military.

GERSON
National security would be the current catchphrase. I'm here to
speak to you about a contract.

FOSTER
I'm sorry he wasted your time, but we don't do military contracts.

GERSON
Actually, you do.

    Beat.

FOSTER
No. We don't.

GERSON

(*laughing*) There's nothing insidious happening here. To clarify, you *do* do military contracts in the sense that Demetech has a pre-existing contract with the military that has yet to be fulfilled.

GERSON removes a file from his briefcase, sets it down on FOSTER's desk.

FOSTER

(*referring to the file*) Aventa Chemicals? Never heard of it.

GERSON

You should have. You own it. (*beat*) Few years back, Aventa merged with another chemical company, which got bought by a larger conglomerate, which then became a wholly owned subsidiary of –

FOSTER

Demetech.

GERSON

Prior to your … merger. These organizations represent an extensive patent portfolio, the selfsame portfolio you sought to obtain by acquiring Demetech, yes? How many such patents does Demetech now own?

FOSTER

Can't say I'm keeping track.

GERSON

Seven hundred, give or take … nearly twice the number of your closest competitor; over half the total number of existing patents on plants and plant technology – an array of organisms and processes essential to industrial agriculture. Quite a lot of power to put in one man's hands.

FOSTER

Sometimes I wear protective gloves.

GERSON

(*laughing*) Safety first, as they say. (*opening the file, removing some papers*) This is a contract between Aventa and the military to manufacture a chemical defoliant. (*handing the papers to FOSTER*) Our lawyers assure us that the contract still stands.

FOSTER

(*scanning the contract*) A defoliant for what use?

GERSON

Overseas operations.

FOSTER

Specifically?

> *Beat.*

GERSON

Afghanistan.

> *Beat.*

FOSTER

You want to defoliate the fields.

GERSON

Our enemy is funded by opium. Opium grown in poppy fields. Roughly four billion dollars per annum.

FOSTER

But our enemy doesn't tend to these crops. You know who does tend them? Farmers and children. *Impoverished* farmers and children.

GERSON

Those are not our intended targets.

FOSTER

But a certain degree of collateral damage won't keep anyone up at night?

GERSON

Every time our soldiers are killed by an IED or roadside bomb, it was bought and paid for with opium. Senator Jakes is the author of a five-pillar proposal to fight the opium trade. One of those pillars is aerial eradication.

FOSTER

I wish him the best, but Demetech is no longer a chemical company.

GERSON

I'm surprised to hear that, since I happen to know you still manufacture chemicals.

FOSTER

We have ... subsidiaries that produce a narrow range of chemical products ... but these are pesticides and herbicides with specific –

GERSON

That's what a defoliant is, is it not? A kind of herbicide?

FOSTER

I'm in the business of growing plants, Mr. Gerson, not destroying them.

GERSON

You took over these companies, you inherited their contracts.

    Beat.

FOSTER

Look, no disrespect to Senator Jakes, but fighting opium through defoliation is like fighting cancer by shaving your legs.

GERSON

(*laughing*) That's a good one!

FOSTER

There's a different way, a *better* way of doing this –

GERSON

I'll remember that one!

FOSTER

Afghanistan has no economy but for this one crop. The West needs opium; we need it for morphine. We already pay other countries to grow poppies for us. Transfer those contracts to the farmers in Afghanistan.

GERSON

Afghan farmers double-crop the fields. There's an opium crop *and* a heroin crop.

FOSTER

And currently your enemy has a monopoly on both.

GERSON

And monopolies are tricky beasts, aren't they, Foster? Demetech, for example, has grown very big very fast. The Justice Department may be persuaded that your patent portfolio constitutes monopoly control of the agriculture industry.

FOSTER

In other words, if I refuse –

GERSON

We could close down your party quick as blinking.

FOSTER

You really think Jakes wants to kill the company that's saving Africa?

GERSON

We're all real impressed with your charity toward Africa, but we also know that Africa opens the door to heavily subsidized no-bid government contracts. Quid pro quo: this is where you make your money. You want Demetech to survive intact to make payday, then do the right thing here.

Long pause.

FOSTER

I don't do military contracts.

GERSON

I'll ask you to reconsider.

FOSTER

I don't reconsider.

FOSTER tosses the contract at GERSON.

Beat.

GERSON picks up the contract and replaces it in the file. He puts the file into his briefcase.

GERSON

What do you think your father would say if he knew you had refused to come to your country's aid in a time of war?

FOSTER

My father?

GERSON

Your father is Norris Bryant?

FOSTER

Was. My adoptive father, yes.

GERSON

He worked on Operation Trail Dust, did he not?

FOSTER

He did. My dad helped make Agent Orange. (*beat*) Norris was a young chemistry major at the University of Chicago who thought he was saving the world. He foresaw an awesome utopia in which whole crops could be produced over several days; scientists working arm in arm with government to provide safe, fast, affordable food. Vietnam, to his mind, was a tangent. A research opportunity. But once he saw what they did with his work ... when he came face to face with the aftermath ... he was so horrified that he quit chemistry, quit science, for good. (*beat*) See, for some of us, our career is our life – when one ends, so does the other. So I think his answer to your question might be: Go fuck yourself.

GERSON exits. AVA enters.

AVA

He seemed huffy.

FOSTER

I need you to find someone ... someone from Aventa Chemicals.

AVA

Where is the company based out of?

FOSTER

It's based out of here. It's us.

AVA

It is?

FOSTER

Find someone who worked for Aventa that might still be kicking around. Bring me a name.

AVA

Okay.

FOSTER

I'm going to need Duncan to head down to the archives, dig through some old contracts.

AVA

Okay. Anything else?

FOSTER

Yeah. Where the hell is Cole?

COLE enters.

COLE

You told my friend to go fuck himself?

FOSTER

You want to go there with me right now?

AVA exits.

COLE

Okay, I get that you're pissed.

FOSTER

Oh, you got that just then?

COLE

The hell happened with Gerson?

FOSTER

You know what, let's skip the exposition and smash-cut straight to where you explain to me why in the fuck I just had that meeting.

COLE

Take a deep breath and understand that I don't know what you're talking about.

FOSTER

You set me up.

COLE

What?

FOSTER

You sent in your guy, your buddy; snuck him in under the radar –

COLE

Wait, what did he want?

FOSTER

You don't know?

COLE

No.

FOSTER

You really don't?

COLE

You – what? – you don't believe me?

FOSTER

We have a deal, right?

COLE

Me and you?

FOSTER

We have a deal. We've always had a deal. From day one we said –
we agreed – we don't do military contracts. We never will. Military
contracts are something we just don't do, right?

COLE

Right. Yes. We have a deal.

FOSTER

So why does your buddy claim I owe the army a defoliant? Threaten
to dissolve my company if I don't?

COLE

The fuck should I know?

FOSTER

He's not your contact? You're not still connected?

COLE

I have friends from the military – Gerson among them – but I
wouldn't say I'm connected.

AVA appears at the door.

AVA

Your wife is on the phone.

FOSTER

Not now.

AVA

She sounds upset.

COLE

Foster, take the –

FOSTER

Not now, I said!

    Beat.

    AVA exits.

COLE

I've seen Gerson all of three times in the past ten years. We served together, but we don't, like, hang out on weekends and play Frisbee or whatever. He asked me if he could meet with you. Whatever he's after, I didn't get a heads-up.

    Beat.

FOSTER

Aventa Chemicals.

COLE

What about it?

FOSTER

You've heard of it?

COLE

Sure. We own it ... or some version of it.

FOSTER

Why don't I know this?

COLE

Because there are things you don't know; things you don't want to know – *ask* not to know. Because you're the ideas guy. You have a vision and other people implement it. There are designers of ditches and diggers of ditches, and we know which one of us is which, right?

FOSTER

Gerson says Aventa was under contract to produce a defoliant for the military. A contract we've now inherited.

COLE

A defoliant for what?

FOSTER

Afghanistan.

COLE

Now I get why you're pissed.

FOSTER

Personally, I'm not keen to unleash another Agent Orange on the world.

COLE

This contract, did he show it to you?

FOSTER

Yes.

COLE

He left a copy?

> *Beat.*

FOSTER

No.

COLE

I'll talk to Duncan. We'll sort it out.

FOSTER

It's a growth hormone. Agent Orange. Tells the plant to grow too
much too fast. Is that what happened here, Cole? To our company?

COLE

You made this grain. We found the capital, acquired the patents;
we made your vision a reality. And when reality wouldn't line up
with that vision – when a company didn't want to get bought, like
Demetech – we found another way. It was a *hostile* takeover.

FOSTER

I know what it was.

COLE

The victims of conquest aren't so keen on the conqueror. They
don't let you in on all the pesky little secrets … like pre-existing
military contracts.

FOSTER

Why didn't we see this coming?

COLE

We knew Aventa was bound to be a minefield. You can see it coming
and still get your leg blown off.

FOSTER

Are there any other contracts we don't know about?

COLE

I'll touch base with Duncan. We'll figure it out.

FOSTER

We've worked so hard to get this far …

COLE

I'll find Gerson, smooth things over.

FOSTER

Fuck that guy.

COLE

Foster, our grain is being shipped on military aircraft. We need the government on side.

Beat.

FOSTER

The last time I saw Norris he was drunk, alone, in the dark, talking to himself ... I tried to take him up to bed, but he pushed me off. Wouldn't budge. I gave up and sat on the floor. Just sat there with him. At one point I realized I was holding on to the cuff of his pants – something I hadn't done since I was a little kid. He leaned over and whispered: "They don't know what I know. They can't." What do you think he meant by that?

COLE

I'm not sure I could say.

Beat.

FOSTER

Maybe we should put Africa on hold.

COLE

Foster –

FOSTER

Just to be sure.

COLE

Sure about what?

FOSTER

Sure our seed is safe.

COLE

Is this about the quote? Mozambique? The poison thing?

Beat.

FOSTER

Susan Farmer. Her baby ... this tiny little girl ... (*beat*) She had no eyes. Sockets, with skin ... but no eyes.

COLE

How old is Mrs. Farmer?

FOSTER

Forties? Late forties?

COLE

Was this her first child?

FOSTER

She'd had five, she said. Five healthy kids.

COLE

Defects are more common in women close to fifty. The risks increase the more children they have. This has nothing to do with us, Foster. She's angry and she's –

FOSTER

Throwing rocks? (*beat*) I want to talk to a scientist. I want to talk to a scientist who knows better than us. (*beat*) I want to talk to Sampson.

COLE

No way.

FOSTER

Where is he?

COLE

On the receiving end of even more severe an ass-fucking than he gave us for all the fuck I care.

FOSTER

Find him. Bring him in.

COLE

You recall the thing with the box, right? That six-month shitstorm? Everyone out for our scalps?

FOSTER

You know that box had nothing to do with us. It was just bad timing.

COLE

Totally bullshit move.

FOSTER

If there's a problem with our grain, he'll know.

COLE

Foster, I'm begging you – anyone but Sampson.

AVA enters.

AVA

I found a name – someone who used to work for Aventa and might still be here.

FOSTER

Yes?

AVA

Sampson Pai.

COLE

Fuck me.

AVA

He was head of R&D for Aventa. But … *does* he still work here?

COLE

Foster, we're not legally allowed to talk to him, much less haul him in against his will.

FOSTER

I won't tell if you don't.

COLE

He's been quarantined for a reason, Foster. If you break the seal on this –

FOSTER

(*to AVA*) Get him here. As soon a possible.

AVA

Do you know where he is?

FOSTER

No.

AVA

Where should I look?

FOSTER/COLE

Strip clubs.

AVA

Ugh.

> *Exits.*

COLE

That guy is like herpes. The sores come and go but you're infected forever. (*beat*) Listen … are we cool?

FOSTER
Yeah.

COLE
Your father would be proud of you. You know that, right?

ISOBEL enters.

ISOBEL
Aren't you boys a little old for strip clubs?

COLE
Isobel, forgive me, I've been meaning to congratulate you. For the baby. I couldn't be happier for you. For both of you.

Beat.

ISOBEL
Thank you for saying so.

COLE exits. ISOBEL falls into FOSTER's arms.

ISOBEL
Love me.

FOSTER
I love you.

ISOBEL
Tell me I am beautiful.

FOSTER
You're beautiful.

ISOBEL
Bring me the basket. I must throw up.

FOSTER fetches the wastebasket.

ISOBEL

No. It passed. I must sit.

He drops the basket and brings her a chair. She sits.

ISOBEL

It is twins.

Beat.

FOSTER

What?

ISOBEL

Our baby turns out to be babies. Two babies. Twins.

FOSTER

He's sure?

ISOBEL

So he says.

FOSTER

Isobel, that's –

ISOBEL

There is a problem.

Beat.

FOSTER

What problem?

ISOBEL

I do not know. He could not say. Maybe not. He needs more tests.

FOSTER

Wait … back up … what … what did he see? What did he say he saw?

ISOBEL

I don't know, I said. Neither does he.

FOSTER

Isobel, he must have said something.

ISOBEL

He said there is something strange with one of the babies.

FOSTER

Strange? Strange how?

ISOBEL

The ultrasound – there was an image but I could not see … could not
tell. He said "Hmm" then "Ah" and he chewed on the end of his pen.
These signals I could not decode.

FOSTER

He didn't say anything, *nothing* more specific than that?

ISOBEL

He will bring me back for an umbilical blood sampling something.
Another needle! I said – if you stick one more needle in me it better
be today! I will not be his personal pincushion for the rest of this
pregnancy!

FOSTER

You have to go back?

ISOBEL

Yes. Now. Straightaway.

FOSTER

What did he say the test is for?

ISOBEL

It is to check for disability.

FOSTER

Disabilities?

ISOBEL

Or defect.

FOSTER

Isobel, which word did he use?

ISOBEL

Both. Neither. I don't remember.

FOSTER

Did he say ... did he say anything about Down's syndrome or –

ISOBEL

I do not –

FOSTER

Is there anything wrong with its eyes?

ISOBEL

Its eyes? Foster! Do not be so morbid!

She lights a cigarette, takes a couple of puffs.

FOSTER

I really wish you wouldn't do that.

ISOBEL

(*stubbing out the cigarette*) He wants to talk to you. To us – together.
To discuss our options.

FOSTER

Our options?

ISOBEL

Yes, Foster. If there is a defect and we decide not to take it to term, then
we can discuss our options. To keep or not to keep, the baby that is.

FOSTER

We would – what? – get rid of the one and keep the other?

ISOBEL

He said this is one option – selective termination.

FOSTER

You mean abortion.

ISOBEL

A selective abortion. They take a needle – big surprise – and give the one an injection and it dies.

FOSTER

But the other one survives?

ISOBEL

Yes. Foster, yes. We only ever wanted one baby ... one healthy baby. At the very worst we will still be where we wish to be. (*beat*) It is very fast, he says, this test. We will know right away.

FOSTER

It all sounds so ... grotesque.

ISOBEL

It is only a test. Will you come? (*beat*) Foster?

FOSTER

I can't.

ISOBEL

We will speak with the doctor. Both of us. You will not sit here and stew.

FOSTER

I ... I can't.

ISOBEL

Foster, please!

FOSTER

I have a meeting.

ISOBEL

Goddammit! Cancel this one and come with me!

FOSTER

Isobel, it's about Africa.

ISOBEL

This is about your child … your children.

FOSTER

If it was any other –

ISOBEL

Which means more?

FOSTER

What?

ISOBEL

The children you must tend to in Africa, or those you have before you here?

FOSTER

You can't possibly ask me to –

ISOBEL

Who is attending this meeting? Who is this saviour of Africa?

Beat.

FOSTER

Gilroy.

ISOBEL

Gilroy? Vandalia Gilroy? That insane vegetarian lady you are feuding with on the Internet?

FOSTER
She's a biochemist.

ISOBEL
What can she possibly have to do with Africa?

FOSTER
I have a plan. (*beat*) I think I have a plan.

ISOBEL
Clearly you have your priorities.

> *AVA enters.*

AVA
Dr. Gilroy is here.

FOSTER
Please show her in.

> *AVA exits.*

ISOBEL
Foster, look at me. (*beat*) All will be well. Doctors know some stuff about some things and almost nothing about anything else. (*beat*) Remember, my handsome, sexy beefcake: you are the good guys.

FOSTER
We know.

> *AVA enters with GILROY.*

AVA
Dr. Gilroy, this is Dr. Bryant.

FOSTER
How do you do?

GILROY
Very well. Thank you, Dr. Bryant.

FOSTER

. Can I offer you something to drink?

GILROY

A glass of water, if you please.

AVA exits.

FOSTER

Allow me to introduce my wife, Isobel.

ISOBEL

I am so very pleased to meet you.

GILROY

You are pregnant.

Beat.

ISOBEL

Yes. How did you know?

GILROY

You're starting to show.

ISOBEL

Am I?

GILROY

My congratulations. I wish for you both the most beautiful, healthy baby.

ISOBEL

Thank you. (*beat*) I have an appointment, I must not be late. Ciao!

ISOBEL exits.

GILROY

Is everything all right?

FOSTER

Pardon me?

GILROY

With the pregnancy?

Beat.

FOSTER

Everything's fine.

GILROY

I don't mean to pry.

AVA enters. She gives GILROY a glass of water.

GILROY

Thank you kindly.

FOSTER

Where are we at, Ava? Me and Dr. Gilroy. How many hits?

AVA

Two hundred thousand.

FOSTER

Since this morning?

GILROY

Evidently our debate has struck a chord.

FOSTER

Looks like.

AVA exits.

GILROY

Thank you for agreeing to participate. Of all the invitations sent to CEOs of biotech firms, you were the only one to accept.

FOSTER

Always happy to stumble blindly into the lion's den. I don't think it
was made clear to me that you intended to post our debate online.

GILROY

No? (*beat*) This is a very big building you have.

FOSTER

We completed construction a few weeks back. Sorting out odds and
ends. Decorating.

GILROY

(*referring to the Rubens painting*) Will most of your decorations be
so portentous?

FOSTER

Eye of the beholder.

GILROY

Here our paths cross for the second time in as many weeks. I must
admit – I'm very curious to know why you asked me here.

FOSTER

I want you to know, first and foremost, that I do not consider you an
enemy. We're passionate about our beliefs, and though those beliefs
may clash, they are nonetheless sincere.

GILROY

You are softening me for something. Or positioning yourself. There is
no need. Please, speak your mind.

   Beat.

FOSTER

I need your help.

GILROY

In what way?

FOSTER
    With Africa.

        Beat.

GILROY
    In what way?

FOSTER
    I need you to speak to the governments of Zambia, Zimbabwe,
    and Mozambique, to their delegates, and declare your support for
    Golden Grain.

GILROY
    But I do not support this grain.

FOSTER
    That's why I need *your* support specifically. It's the only way to
    change their minds. They trust you. If you tell them to accept the aid,
    they will.

GILROY
    There are fifty-three countries in Africa. If three reject your grain, you
    will still have succeeded with fifty.

FOSTER
    I need them all. Every country. Every country must accept.

GILROY
    But why?

FOSTER
    If three decline – if *one* declines – then *that's* the story. That's what
    the media reports. That's what the public remembers.

GILROY
    You wish to alter the narrative.

FOSTER

I want to prevent millions from turning their backs on salvation.

GILROY

There are many starving people in the world. Is it your intent to save them all?

FOSTER

Yes. Will you help me?

Beat.

GILROY

I'm sorry, I cannot.

FOSTER

I must ask you to reconsider.

GILROY

It is impossible.

FOSTER

Please?

GILROY

It is not you I will not help. It is this – your corporation.

FOSTER

We're one and the same.

GILROY

Not at all! You – Foster Bryant – are a human being. You know love and friendship; you hold passionate beliefs, as you said. Soon you will know the joy of children. Your corporation – Demetech – is an entity. It has no feelings, no beliefs, no moral responsibilities. It is beholden only to itself.

FOSTER

We will strike a balance between capitalism and compassion.

GILROY

These are contradictory motives. Eventually one must supersede the other.

FOSTER

I will use Demetech as a force for good. As a means to an end.

GILROY

It may do good by virtue – by coincidence or accident – but you cannot make it do good deeds, only profitable ones. You may want to save lives, but the entity must profit from the saving of those lives. Somewhere down the line, someone must pay.

FOSTER

You're right. Demetech must make money. The company profits from selling the seed to those who can afford it, and for those who can't – it will be free.

GILROY

More difficult, perhaps, to sell your grain to those who can pay if those who can't refuse, no? (*beat*) Your chemicals – those required to treat the crop – these too are free?

FOSTER

Yes. Of course.

GILROY

At first. And when it spreads, when these crops contaminate others, then these farmers must pay for the privilege of growing your grain?

FOSTER

We build buffer zones to prevent contamination.

GILROY

By "contamination" you mean stop pollen from spreading? Surely, as a scientist, you know this is absurd. Such is the purpose of pollen – to spread!

FOSTER

We will still have given people with no food the means to grow food forever. The seed self-pollinates – a perfect crop each and every time!

GILROY

Your food, *your* seed. The grain your company made and owns. Once it starts to spread – how long? How long until your rice is the only rice we have? Then what? Your corn? Your wheat? How long until we depend on you for all the food we eat?

FOSTER

Would you choose to starve instead?

GILROY

There is more at stake than eating or not eating.

FOSTER

We have the luxury to make that distinction.

GILROY

Luxury? Not at all! To safeguard our most basic rights.

FOSTER

Cold comfort on an empty stomach.

GILROY

You control seed, you control food; you control food, you control people. Better than guns and bombs by far. (*beat*) Seed was once regarded as too essential, too sacred to be bought and sold. But if you upend the norm – now seed is property – what stops you from owning life itself? You own many patents on plants and bacteria already ... why not animals?

FOSTER

But what could my endgame possibly be? What would I do with all this control? So I own all life on earth. What on earth do I do with all that life?

GILROY

It's obvious – you profit! I own the rights to this fish or that cow –
pay up!

FOSTER

That's preposterous.

GILROY

To the contrary, it is the next logical step for the entity to take
because it is precisely how the entity charts its course – by the route
that offers the most possible gain. To be fair, this may not interest
you. But when you are gone – when you have left or your board has
fired you – who is in charge?

FOSTER

You see the world through conspiratorial eyes – puppets and masters
and a maze of string. You mock my methods, heap scorn on my
company – the font of every global ill. I am become death, the
destroyer of worlds.

GILROY

Set your methods and company aside. We assume your intentions
are entirely altruistic, an even more central dilemma remains: No one
knows if your seed is safe.

FOSTER

It is.

GILROY

So you say.

FOSTER

Can you tell me how my seed is *unsafe*?

GILROY

In India, one of your competitors sold farmers GMO seeds for
cotton. They are suicide seeds – the cotton grows the first season
but cannot be replanted. These seeds contaminated many crops. The

farmers cannot afford new seeds every season, so now the farmers kill themselves. They lose their livelihood. Land that has been in their family for generations – spoiled.

FOSTER

I don't make seeds for cotton. I don't make suicide seeds.

GILROY

I speak of consequences, Dr. Bryant, both foreseen and unforeseen. This is no conspiracy. Those farmers have been abandoned.

FOSTER

As you would abandon the citizens of Zambia, Zimbabwe, and Mozambique?

GILROY

It is convenient for you – as a person of privilege – to speak so stridently.

FOSTER

I was adopted into a family of privilege, that is true. But don't think I don't know what it means to be abandoned.

GILROY

Foster Bryant, son of Norris, he who helped defoliate Vietnam. Now you want to save the world. Atone, perhaps, for your father's sins. You are dissatisfied with how this chapter is turning out, and you want to rewrite. Me, your co-author! What an unlikely pair we make.

FOSTER

You came out against this technology early and eagerly and – I've got to hand it to you – you're famous because of it. Speaking tours, books, television … You're a martyr and a folk hero, saving the world from us evil corporate overlords.

GILROY

I am a scientist first and foremost.

FOSTER

Are you?

GILROY

I ran the first clinical trials on GMO foods. We fed modified potatoes to rats, and the mucosal thickness of the stomach lining indicated that the immune system regarded the food as alien.

FOSTER

You speak out, you're fired, your project is disbanded ... I've read your biography.

GILROY

I was humiliated. Intentionally. To discredit my work. To distract public attention from the findings of my research.

FOSTER

We replicated your trials ten times over.

GILROY

Did you? (*beat*) And? What did you find?

FOSTER

The science has *improved*. See, here's the difference between me and you: you've devoted your life to fighting this technology while I've devoted mine to fixing it.

GILROY

And now? Is it fixed?

FOSTER

We've run the experiments, gone above and beyond government regulations, industry standards –

GILROY

You know of no potential hazards in distributing your grain?

FOSTER

No.

GILROY

You – do you eat it?

FOSTER

And if I did? Or didn't? Would that make the difference?

GILROY

Tell me, do you?

FOSTER

Would that be proof enough? If I said yes – so certain am I of its safety that I eat it myself – would you speak to these nations? To their delegates?

GILROY

You have not answered my question.

FOSTER

You haven't answered mine. (*beat*) You wouldn't, would you? You're so convinced. (*beat*) If they don't accept the aid, people will die. That is a foreseen consequence. Guaranteed.

GILROY

So you said.

FOSTER

Children will die.

GILROY

It saddens me to say so, but that is their choice.

FOSTER

Whose choice?

GILROY

The people of –

FOSTER

The people or their government?

GILROY

These are democratic nations. The people are the –

FOSTER

Surely you aren't that naive.

GILROY

You cannot force your food down their throats!

FOSTER

Not because you know this food isn't safe, but only because you want it not to be.

GILROY

I speak the truth.

FOSTER

As you see it.

GILROY

Yes! As I see it!

FOSTER

(*quoting GILROY's words from the opening scene*) "You see only what you want to see, look only for what you want to find."

GILROY

Better than you! Better than your blind faith in your poisonous seed!

FOSTER

Poisonous seed … (*beat*) This isn't about my grain, or my company, or me. You want to be right. You've staked everything on your certitude – your reputation, your livelihood, your fame – and you're willing to let whole populations perish so that you won't be proven wrong.

GILROY

It is not my fault these people are starving! I am no partisan. It is not my place to play politics. If they reject your aid, so be it! My hands are clean!

FOSTER

Who told her that the food is poison?

Beat.

GILROY

Pardon me?

FOSTER

The prime minister of Mozambique. Who told her that the food is poison? Who planted *that* seed? (*beat*) That quote, that idea, is the reason those countries turned me down. And I think it came from you. Am I wrong? (*beat*) Am I? (*beat*) Poison. Based on what evidence? What proof? What science? And you accuse me of blind faith. (*beat*) Let's be blunt, Vandalia – you abandoned science a long time ago. Now you're a pundit, a street preacher ... Every demagogue has a niche market nowadays and you're milking yours for all it's worth. (*beat*) Be honest. This is just as much a business opportunity for you as it is for me.

Long pause.

GILROY

If I speak to these nations, to their delegates, you must do something for me in return.

FOSTER

Oh, we're bartering now?

GILROY

Stay out of India.

FOSTER

There are lots of starving people in India.

GILROY

I know this all too well, but we must find another way. We like our rice the way it is.

Beat.

FOSTER extends his hand. GILROY shakes it.

GILROY
Good day.

FOSTER
Same to you.

GILROY exits. AVA enters.

FOSTER
Contact the board. Tell them that the holdouts are a go.

AVA
All three?

FOSTER
The governments of Zambia, Zimbabwe, and Mozambique are about to have a change of heart.

AVA
You're kidding!

FOSTER
I'm not.

AVA
You're a genius!

FOSTER
I am. It's true.

AVA
Foster, that's fantastic!

FOSTER
I'll call Paul personally. Notify Duncan and Cole …

AVA

I'm on it. (*beat*) Oh, I found him!

FOSTER

Found who?

AVA

Sampson!

FOSTER

At a club?

AVA

He was. He's here.

FOSTER

Bring him in. (*beat*) Good job, Ava.

AVA moves to the door.

AVA

Mr. Pai, if you'd like to come in …

SAMPSON enters – clearly drunk.

SAMPSON

Foster, what's up?

FOSTER

Long time no see.

SAMPSON

No doubt. Not since the trial. Thanks for the generous settlement, brother. I keep up my end of the bargain …

He makes a zipper motion across his mouth.

FOSTER

My pleasure.

SAMPSON

Summoned to the tip of the ivory tower. I'm not worthy!

FOSTER

Busy these days?

SAMPSON

I was eye deep in tits and had the better part of a rum and Coke on the go, so ...

FOSTER

Ava, bring Sampson a glass of water.

SAMPSON

Scotch, actually.

AVA

Sure.

SAMPSON

Single malt, neat.

> AVA *exits.*

FOSTER

You good?

SAMPSON

Grand, my man.

FOSTER

Still living out of the clubs?

SAMPSON

Only way to wind down.

FOSTER

On my dime?

SAMPSON

That's life in limbo. Can't hire me, can't fire me! Let's make a deal!

AVA enters with a glass of water. She hands it to SAMPSON.

SAMPSON

She's fast! What was your name? Ava?

(sings)

Show a little skin, make a little cash – get down tonight!
Aow!

AVA exits.

SAMPSON

She's smokin'. You been all up ons that shit or what?

FOSTER

I miss you, Sampson.

SAMPSON

Honey bear! I miss you too. I don't even remember what we were
fighting about.

FOSTER

You sent a box of documents to a reporter.

SAMPSON

Oh yeah.

FOSTER

Internal documents.

SAMPSON

I did indeed.

FOSTER

Confidential internal documents.

SAMPSON

Big box too.

FOSTER

You set us back the better part of half a year.

SAMPSON

You still sore?

Beat.

FOSTER

You did what you thought was right.

SAMPSON

Wasn't personal. I didn't even know you, bro. My old superiors, the prior regime, they're the ones who wouldn't come clean. I took an oath, right? At least I think I did. I find something wrong, I speak up. But they would not pick up what I laid down, dig? I was revised, redacted ... severed with the stroke of a Sharpie. By the time your team rolled in, the big bad box was already in the mail and that cat was *way* out of the bag. Bad luck it was your face got scratched up.

FOSTER

You dropped the box before I bought Demetech; it exploded after. I get it; I'm not pointing fingers.

SAMPSON

None of us knew the company was even on the block. Then, after the takeover, well ... shit just got tense.

FOSTER

Why didn't you come to me?

SAMPSON

I sent up a few flares ... But you, I mean – you're insulated.

FOSTER

We saw each other two or three times a day.

SAMPSON

Yeah but I didn't know you. Hey new boss man, I just busted old boss man for fraud and conspiracy. Nice to meet you!

FOSTER

Okay –

SAMPSON

I never wanted to be Corporate Espionage Deep Throat Guy. I do what you do – I run tests. I find something wrong, I say so – in my own way.

FOSTER

And now? What? Stalemate?

SAMPSON

Don't blame me, blame whistleblower protection legislation. (*beat*) Is this why you brought me here? Relive the golden olden days? Because, y'know, no hard feelings, but I'd rather be nose deep in poonani.

FOSTER

Our chemicals – our pesticide and herbicide blends – can they cause reproductive disorders?

SAMPSON

Not that I know of.

FOSTER

Birth defects?

SAMPSON

Nope.

FOSTER

Embryo? Fetus? Nothing?

Beat.

SAMPSON

This is in regards to what?

FOSTER

There's a woman, a farmer ... she claims our chemicals caused one of her children to be born with a severe deformity.

SAMPSON

What kind of deformity?

FOSTER

I'd rather not –

SAMPSON

What kind of deformity?

Beat.

FOSTER

The child has no eyes.

SAMPSON

I see. (*beat*) I *see*. (*beat*) Wow, tough room. She started applying them when?

FOSTER

Three years ago.

SAMPSON

Nothing to do with the chemicals.

FOSTER

You're sure?

SAMPSON

Our chemicals are safe – the new blends – relatively. As far as, you
know, a necessary evil, they're pretty benign. The likelihood that
they would cause birth defects is so low it would be considered
statistically insignificant.

FOSTER

This defect was definitely not caused by our chemicals?

SAMPSON

Definitely not the chemicals.

FOSTER

Good, that's all I needed to –

SAMPSON

It's the crop.

> *Beat.*

FOSTER

What?

SAMPSON

The rice itself. Golden Grain.

> *Beat.*

FOSTER

What?

SAMPSON

Her field was next to a test crop, right? It was contaminated?

FOSTER

How did you know that?

SAMPSON

It's the hybrids. The hybrids cause the defects.

FOSTER

Wait, that can't be right.

SAMPSON

The seed self-pollinates, the genetic code is locked. But the plants still produce pollen, that pollen still spreads, still fertilizes other plants. That's where shit gets sticky.

FOSTER

But we ran those tests – Sampson, I know we ran those tests – on the grain *and* the hybrids. We looked specifically at females, at pregnancies, for abnormalities. We didn't find anything!

SAMPSON

Not in the women, no. Seems natural to look at the women – original sin, right? But it ain't Eve; it's Adam. It's the men, son. It's the sperm.

FOSTER

The sperm?

SAMPSON

I know – real swift kick to the sack, eh? In those trials, the hybrid trials, female subjects were fine ... I mean they reproduced fine provided they were mated with control-group males. But when we mated test males with control females – when we mated test males with *any* females – there was a spike in the number of defects. (*beat*) You should come see my jars.

FOSTER

Your what?

SAMPSON

I have quite the collection – a formaldehyde freak show of genetic up-fucks. Animals born without eyes, limbs, teeth, joints, genitalia – without or with extra. You name it, I seen it.

FOSTER

You're telling me that males who were fed hybrid strains of Golden Grain produced offspring with a higher rate of birth defects?

SAMPSON

Yes, and ...

FOSTER

"And"? (*beat*) "And" what?!

SAMPSON

And it's locked.

FOSTER

Locked? What do you mean "locked"?

SAMPSON

If that deformed child has children, those offspring will be born with the selfsame deformity. The deformities are self-replicating, like the grain, locked inside the code.

FOSTER

(*to himself*) Said she wouldn't touch the stuff ... said her husband ate it ...

SAMPSON

Not that I'm clear on how much action the average gimp gets.

FOSTER grabs SAMPSON, shakes him.

FOSTER

WHY DIDN'T YOU TELL ME?!

SAMPSON

Hey! Easy!

AVA appears at the door. COLE is with her.

FOSTER

Why didn't you tell me?

AVA

Foster!

SAMPSON

It was all in my reports! But then the Sharpie is unsheathed ... First
it's just a tweak or two, but the next thing you know, the molecular
structure itself has been forever altered ...

FOSTER

Someone changed your reports?

COLE

Foster, let him go.

FOSTER releases SAMPSON.

SAMPSON

And they say you're just a stuffed shirt ...

FOSTER

You knew there was a problem, you knew your reports were being
tampered with, and you still didn't come to me?

SAMPSON

You're saving Africa! Who gets between the fat kid and that Smartie?
Not me. No way. Then the thing with the box ... Like anyone was
gonna listen to the guy who just pissed all over the rug. People
wouldn't even look me in the eye!

FOSTER

What percentage?

COLE

Foster, shut this down.

FOSTER

By what percentage do the incidents of defects increase?

COLE

Ava, call security.

AVA rushes out.

SAMPSON

Zero-point-five percent, give or take.

FOSTER

That's it?

SAMPSON

"That's it"? Yeah, Foster – that's it. An increase one might call statistically insignificant. That's what it says in my reports. Statistically insignificant ... Sounds pretty, well, insignificant, doesn't it? But once your seed starts to spread, take over other crops – and we're talking exponentially, right? – instead of millions, it's a billion people eating your rice – what's point-five percent of that? And that's just the first generation. Then they start to fuck each other. You know they will – that's what we do! – we fuck each other!

COLE shoves SAMPSON.

COLE

You want to talk about getting fucked?

COLE shoves him again.

SAMPSON

I set you back six months? My whole life burned down! My trial wasn't even over by the time you guys were back in business. (*to FOSTER*) And where were you? Where were you? It's not that you weren't asking the right questions, Foster. You weren't asking any!

FOSTER
Get out.

SAMPSON
Here's some advice, since I'm still on salary: in my professional scientific opinion, you tell those Africans to build a bigger buffer zone. You tell them to build the *biggest* buffer zone!

FOSTER
GET OUT!

AVA enters with a SECURITY GUARD.

Beat.

SAMPSON
Cool by me. I'm heading back to the club … just in time for amateur hour. That's when the fur really starts to fly!

SAMPSON hands his glass to AVA.

SAMPSON
Weak-ass motherfuckin' Scotch, yo.

SAMPSON exits with the SECURITY GUARD.

FOSTER
Ava, get Paul on the line.

COLE
Hold on.

FOSTER
We're putting Africa on hold.

COLE
Foster, wait –

FOSTER
Ava, now!

COLE

Ava, stop! Give us a minute.

Beat.

AVA exits.

COLE

You can't put Africa on hold.

FOSTER

Don't tell me what I can and cannot do.

COLE

You can't put Africa on hold.

FOSTER

It is poison. Our grain. That woman … her baby … We contaminated her field. Her husband was eating it. Sampson's tests –

COLE

Fuck Sampson.

FOSTER

Someone altered the language in his –

COLE

Yes. I did.

Beat.

FOSTER

You marked the spike in defects as statistically insignificant?

COLE

Actually, I only added the "in."

FOSTER

Why?

COLE

Because it is. Point-five percent? Who gives a fuck?

FOSTER

The code is locked.

COLE

So Sampson says.

FOSTER

It was his research! He wrote those reports!

COLE

And did you read them? (*beat*) Did you?

FOSTER

Our seed isn't safe.

COLE

The planes are on the tarmac.

FOSTER

We have to call it off.

COLE

We've spent hundreds of millions to get to this point.

FOSTER

So we'll spend a few million more.

COLE

There isn't another million to spend.

FOSTER

We'll find more money. We always find more money.

COLE

I always find more money.

FOSTER

So … are you saying you couldn't, or you wouldn't bother?

COLE

Foster, how do we make money?

Beat.

FOSTER

What?

COLE

How do you – Foster Bryant – think we – Demetech – make money?

Beat.

FOSTER

Selling seed. Selling the chemicals to treat that seed.

COLE

That's how we *will* make money, but how do you think we make money *now*? As in today.

Beat.

FOSTER

What's the difference?

COLE

The seed is an idea. An idea we've developed but have yet to deploy. The value of our stock, our company, of this entire enterprise is grounded in the future viability of that idea.

FOSTER

I don't understand.

COLE

We don't make money. Or … we haven't yet.

FOSTER

I'm … lost … Cole, I don't –

COLE

When you took over Demetech we left all other pursuits behind.
Everything is Golden Grain. Everything is Africa.

FOSTER

But we report our profits every quarter. Our stock is going up,
you said –

COLE

It's called mark-to-market accounting. You have an idea, and I predict
the profit that that idea will generate. Then we put the potential
profit on the books as actual profit.

FOSTER

How do you predict the profit for a project that hasn't happened yet?

COLE

I guess.

FOSTER

That isn't illegal?

COLE

Not if your accountant says it isn't. (*beat*) Once Africa is under way,
our government contracts kick in. When our contracts kick in, we
make money.

FOSTER

But those profits are already on the books?

COLE

Yes.

FOSTER

Since when?

COLE

Since the day Africa was announced. That was when the idea became a reality.

FOSTER

And if Africa doesn't happen, then the company ... what ... ?

COLE

Implodes. We're a husk. Then there's a hole in the ground.

FOSTER

You ... You fucked us.

COLE

Did I? Perspective really is everything, isn't it? See, from my vantage point, I *made* us. But then, that's what I like about me and you ... that tacit agreement. You live your life in a goddamn snow globe and every so often I give it a good shake so that you can run around screaming "Blizzard!"

FOSTER

Which means more?

COLE

Are you asking me if I care about Africa ... about Africans? Well no, I don't. But you do, so I don't have to. (*beat*) Break it down – for every hundred people you save, one will suffer. *Might* suffer. That's the trade-off. Not only will no one care, no one will notice. (*beat*) And we both know the truth, right? Every starving African you feed today makes two starving Africans you need to feed tomorrow. We're only prolonging the inevitable. (*goes to the door and opens it*) Come on in.

GERSON enters.

COLE

Sorry to keep you waiting.

GERSON

Must be a very busy day for both of you. I really do appreciate your time.

COLE

Don't mention it.

GERSON

I'm sorry, Mr. Bryant, if we got off on the wrong foot earlier. (*beat*) I heard what you said … about transferring opium contracts to Afghan farmers. I think the idea has merit and I'll mention it to my superiors. I'll make sure they hear me on that. Provided you and I start at square one.

COLE

We want to cooperate. We want to do what's in everyone's best interests.

GERSON

Glad to hear it.

COLE

We need to give our lawyers some time to look over these contracts, the nature of our obligations here; then we'll do our best to honour them.

GERSON

You both agree on this?

COLE

Yes.

GERSON

Both of you?

> FOSTER *says nothing.*

GERSON

This contract notwithstanding, the military expended significant resources on Aventa, resources that benefited your company as a whole. Not just chemicals, but a slew of technologies now owned by Demetech.

FOSTER

What are you saying?

GERSON

I'm saying you're eating pie we paid to bake. Shouldn't we all get a slice?

FOSTER

You want – what? – money? You want your cut?

COLE

This isn't about money, Foster. What he wants is a relationship.

GERSON

We want access to your patents for our own research, our own products … You understand?

Beat.

FOSTER

Quid pro quo?

GERSON

Ask away.

FOSTER

We're shipping a hundred thousand tonnes of Golden Grain to Africa today.

GERSON

So you are.

FOSTER

But there's a problem. The hybrid strain leads to increased incidents of birth defects.

GERSON

It's my understanding that the government was informed of a slight uptick in potential defects, but that the increase was determined to be statistically insignificant.

FOSTER

Well, it depends on your metric. Could be a few thousand, could be tens of millions.

COLE

This ... he's ... these are speculations based on the results of preliminary –

FOSTER

And the likelihood is that other crops will be contaminated. So we'll need some cover. Protection from civil and criminal allegations brought against us for any ... unintended consequences resulting from the use of our product.

GERSON

You want immunity from potential litigation?

COLE

Foster –

FOSTER

And criminal charges. In perpetuity.

COLE

Let's put this on the back burner until we've had time to –

GERSON

We're talking Africa?

FOSTER
We're talking everywhere.

Beat.

GERSON
I really don't think it'll be a problem.

Beat.

FOSTER
No?

GERSON
I'm sure we can work something out.

Beat.

FOSTER
You don't think it'll be a problem?

GERSON
Did I stutter?

Beat.

FOSTER
It didn't even faze you.

GERSON
What?

FOSTER
You barely even paused. You really don't care?

GERSON
Care about what?

FOSTER
Collateral damage.

GERSON

Cole, I'm confused –

FOSTER

No, of course you don't.

COLE

Let's stop here and reschedule for another –

FOSTER

What if I'd said a hundred million defects? A billion?

GERSON

That's not what –

FOSTER

"I'm sure we can work something out." That's what you said.

GERSON

Are you winding your way around to some kind of point?

FOSTER

I just want to know the square tonnage of bodies it would take to give you pause. A rough estimate would suffice. Ballpark.

GERSON

You'll want to watch your tone with me.

FOSTER

You'll want to kiss my ass.

GERSON

Whose goddamn planes do you think are flying your fucking rice 'round the world?

    FOSTER picks up the phone.

FOSTER

Ava, get General Keyes on the line. (*to GERSON*) Do you want to shut it down or should I?

He holds out the phone to GERSON.

GERSON

You boys are more fucked than an asshole in Dicktown.

GERSON exits.

COLE

Foster –

FOSTER

It's over.

ISOBEL appears at the door. COLE moves past her, exits.

FOSTER

I'm sorry, Iz, I'm on a call.

ISOBEL lights a cigarette, smokes.

FOSTER

Iz? (*beat*) What are you doing? (*beat*) General, it's Foster. Isobel, put that out.

She smokes. She retrieves her glass of wine.

FOSTER

Put that out right now.

She drinks the wine. She smokes.

FOSTER

General, I'm sorry – could you please hold? One minute.

FOSTER hangs up the phone. He tries to take the cigarette away from Isobel. She keeps it out of his reach.

FOSTER
What is this?

FOSTER grabs the cigarette, stubs it out. She lights another.

FOSTER
Don't mess with me right now.

ISOBEL
You make your calls.

FOSTER takes this cigarette away, stubs it out. She lights another.

FOSTER
Isobel, what is it?

ISOBEL
You need to make your calls, make your calls.

FOSTER
What's wrong with you?

ISOBEL
With it.

FOSTER
"It" what?

ISOBEL
It is deformed.

FOSTER
What?

ISOBEL
What? What?! What do you think? The baby. One of the babies.
One of the babies is deformed.

Beat.

FOSTER

What did the doctor say?

ISOBEL

He said some stuff and some stuff and some –

FOSTER

Isobel, would you tell me in plain fucking English what the doctor –

ISOBEL

I am too old! We knew I was too old. I have been ripe for too long and now withered on the vine. I have expired.

FOSTER

This is what he told you?

ISOBEL

It does not matter what he told me! I know. You say women are having children later and later in life, but that is not right. Science has women have children later and later in life. Women themselves – no.

FOSTER

Isobel –

ISOBEL

You had to know! All these tests – you had to know, had to be sure. Now look! See? Do you see?

FOSTER

Stop.

ISOBEL

You wanted to look! Well? Now? Are you satisfied? You see and are you satisfied?!

Beat.

FOSTER

Could he tell?

ISOBEL
    Tell what?

FOSTER
    The sex?

ISOBEL
    What does it matter?

FOSTER
    It matters to me.

ISOBEL
    No, Foster –

FOSTER
    I want to know.

ISOBEL
    No.

FOSTER
    Tell me.

ISOBEL
    This too?

FOSTER
    Yes!

ISOBEL
    You must? (*beat*) No. I will not tell you. This you will not know.
    (*beat*) We will be rid of it. I will have the injection.

FOSTER
    We have to discuss this.

ISOBEL
    Now we will have a discussion.

FOSTER

I'll speak with the doctor –

ISOBEL

Now you will speak with the doctor.

FOSTER

We'll go over our options.

ISOBEL

You cannot save it! Some things cannot be saved!

FOSTER

This is not your decision and yours alone!

ISOBEL

I am sick of your decisions. They lead only to misery.

FOSTER

What did you just say to me?

ISOBEL

We will be rid of it.

FOSTER

No.

ISOBEL

We will.

FOSTER

No!

ISOBEL

Then I will be rid of it!

FOSTER grabs her.

FOSTER

I said no!

ISOBEL

Let go of me!

ISOBEL wrenches herself from FOSTER's grip. FOSTER grabs her satchel. He dumps the contents onto the tables, grabs the pack of cigarettes, and crushes them in his fist. ISOBEL grabs him and he shoves her, hard. She falls. He tosses the cigarettes to the floor.

AVA is at the door.

Long pause.

ISOBEL

We will kill one and save the other.

ISOBEL exits.

FOSTER

What?

AVA

The general had to go. He told me to tell you that the planes are taking off. The birds are in the air, he said.

AVA exits.

Long pause.

AVA enters.

AVA

She wants me to take her. To the doctor.

Beat.

FOSTER

Go.

Beat.

AVA exits.

FOSTER picks up the phone and dials.

Beat.

FOSTER

(*into phone*) Hello, may I speak to Dr. Brooks please? ... (*listening*) Foster Bryant ... (*listening*) Thank you. (*beat*) Hey Ken, it's Foster ... (*listening*) Yeah, I'm sorry I couldn't be there with her today. (*beat*) How accurate are the results? ... (*listening*) I see. Well, we talked it over, and we've decided to move ahead with selective termination of the deformed twin ... (*listening*) And there's no way the healthy baby will be harmed by this procedure? ... (*listening*) Well, there's always risk ... (*listening*) May I ask what you do with it? The deformed fetus ... ? (*listening*) This may sound strange ... but could it be ... returned to me? ... (*listening*) I understand. I would consider it a ... personal favour ... (*listening*) It may ... prove useful ... in future research.

FOSTER hangs up.

Beat.

ALEX enters.

ALEX

Hello ... ?

FOSTER

Who are you?

ALEX

I'm ... uh ... Alex. Alex Skilling. From ... from *Fortune* magazine?

Beat.

FOSTER

The article.

ALEX

Uh … yeah. Sorry to just wander in … doesn't seem like there's anyone much in the building today.

FOSTER

We're decorating.

ALEX

You're Foster Bryant. (*beat*) Someone called and asked if I could come to see you. (*referring to the painting*) Is that a Rubens?

FOSTER

Take a seat. Get comfortable.

ALEX

I want you to know that I worked really hard on that article. I tried to contact people from your company, but no one seemed to want to talk to me and I had a deadline so we went ahead and published anyway. You should know that I … uh … stand by everything … the factual accuracy of everything I wrote. I studied your financial statements, in detail. Demetech is a black box and I just … I can't for the life of me figure out how your company makes money.

FOSTER

Sit, I said.

ALEX sits.

FOSTER

You like wine?

ALEX

Uh … sure.

FOSTER brings over two glasses of wine, hands one to ALEX.

ALEX

Oh. (*taking a sip*) Ugh.

FOSTER returns to his desk.

FOSTER

There is a plague coming. And I am the epicentre.

ALEX sets down the wine, pulls out a pen and a pad of paper …

Blackout.

End of play.

Acknowledgments

I am indebted to far too many people to name here: actors, designers, directors, and dramaturges whose formidable talents and insights over the course of several read-throughs and workshops had a profound and indelible impact on the development of this play. You know who you are. I owe you big time.

Thanks to Brad Fox, Ross Hodgson, Erin Hoos, Matthew Hoos, Toby Malone, Erin Oke, Eric Rose, Evan Rothery, Amy Lynn Strilchuk, Bryan Wade, and Paula Wing. Your mentorship, counsel, support, and friendship mean everything.

Thanks to the cast and crew – Patrick, Alison, Mia, Carl, Tamara, Dave, Adele, Tetsuro, Dallas, Daniel, Florence, Jergus, Jordan, and everyone at Upintheair Theatre – for their sterling contributions to the premiere production. I remain honoured and humbled by your work. I couldn't have wished for a better initial mounting.

To the director of that premiere, Richard Wolfe: you have my utmost gratitude. You made it better than it was in my head, and that almost never happens.

Huge thanks to everyone at Talonbooks: Kevin, Vicki, Spencer, Jenn, Chloë, and Ann-Marie. It has been a pleasure.

To my stalwart friends and collaborators Daniel Martin and David Mott (in alphabetical order): you saved this piece from the void. I can't thank you enough. Much love.

Jason Patrick Rothery has produced full-length work as a playwright and collaborative-creator, including *the space between us* (Tziporah Productions), *(re)Birth: e. e. cummings in Song* (Soulpepper), *Wedgie* (Upintheair), *Something to Do With Death* and *POLITIkO* (Ghost River), and *The Drop* and *Re:Generation* (THEATREboom). He was the co-creator of The Walking Fish Festival (Vancouver), co-founder and festival director of the Calgary International Fringe Festival, resident playwright of the second Soulpepper Academy, and the erstwhile artistic director of Ghost River Theatre (Calgary), where he mounted dozens of productions and tours including *NiX*, presented as part of the 2010 Cultural Olympiad. He is currently a PhD student in communication studies at Carleton University, where he is studying the discursive construction of agency in video game advertising. He is also adapting China Miéville's celebrated novel *The City and The City* for a co-production between Vancouver-based theatre companies Upintheair and The Only Animal.